Spiralizer Cookbook

40 Amazing and Easy Spiralizer Recipes for

a Healthy Life

(Spiralize Everything Book 1)

By Brendan Fawn

Table of Contents

Spiralized Potatoes Fries with Pineapple

Spiralized Zucchini Noodles Soup with Turkey

Zucchini Pasta Soup with Dried Mushrooms

Inspiralized Carrots with Beef

Spiralized Vegetable Mix

Peanuts and Zucchini Pasta

Zucchini Spaghetti with Avocado

Cream Zucchini Pasta

Pesto, Chicken and Zucchini Pasta

Broccoli and Beets Spaghetti

Beetroot and Squash Pesto Spaghetti

Parsnip Noodles with Sardines

Baked Zucchini Noodles with Buckwheat

Spicy Spiralized Zucchini with Rice

Baked Zucchini Noodles with Beef

Eggplant Spaghetti with Pesto

Spiralized Zucchini with Onions

Spiralized Beetroots with Mackerel

Walnuts and Zucchini Pasta

Beetroots Noodles with Bacon

Kohlrabi Noodles with Beef

Cucumbers Pasta Rolls

Introduction

This spiralizer cookbook was created for those who want to choose a healthier food or just want to try new tastes.

This cookbook includes various spiralizer recipes, such as soups, salads, vegetable pasta, vegetable noodles or hot dishes. In this cookbook, you will find interesting spiralized vegetable recipes that will inspire you to cook fantastic spiralized veggie dishes. Often you should just use your imagination because actually there is no limit what you can cook. This spiralizer cookbook hasn't all the recipes because it was created to inspire you to discover a colorful world of spiralizer cooking! Moreover, you don't need to be a professional 28 Michelin Star chef to use spiralizer recipes from this cookbook and to prepare food for yourself or your family. I would like to encourage you to test new spiralizer recipes and to experiment with vegetables adding your own flavors!

Summer Mix Carrots Strands

 Prep Time: 10 min. | Servings: 2

Ingredients:

2 carrots

5 cherry tomatoes

4 lettuce

2 oz fresh young beet leaves

1 pomegranate seeds

4 tbsp. lime juice

Dressing:

4 tbsp. Olive oil

4 tbsp. soy sauce

salt and pepper

How to Prepare:

1. Peel the carrots and then shred it into strands using a spiralizer and halve the cherry tomatoes.

2. Add the pomegranate seeds and beet leaves and mix in a big bowl.

3. Now let's prepare the dressing - combine the Olive oil, salt, pepper and soy sauce and whisk well.

4. Pour the dressing over the salad, mix well, pour the lime juice, cover the bowl and then place the salad in the fridge for one hour.

Nutritional Information:

Calories: 130

Total fat: 8 oz

Total carbohydrates: 9 oz

Protein: 4 oz

Orange Zucchini Spaghetti

Prep Time: 5 min. | Cooking Time: 10 min. | Servings: 3

Ingredients:

2 oranges, cubed

1 young zucchini, peeled and spiralized

2 cucumbers, peeled and spiralized

half cup peanuts

Dressing:

4 tbsp. white wine vinegar

4 cloves of garlic

5 fresh basil leaves

1 tsp. chili powder

salt

How to Prepare:

1. Roast the peanuts in the oven for 10 min. until lightly browned and crispy.

2. Combine the peanuts with the oranges, cucumbers and zucchini stripes.

3. Let's get to the dressing now – combine the white wine vinegar, garlic, chili powder, salt, and basil and pulse them in a blender until homogenous mass.

4. Mix the dressing with the zucchini and cucumbers spaghetti and sprinkle some peanuts on top!

Nutritional Information:

Calories: 139

Total fat: 9 oz

Total carbohydrates: 15 oz

Protein: 6 oz

Cucumbers Spaghetti

Prep Time: 5 min. | Cooking Time: 5 min. | Servings: 2

Ingredients:

2 cucumbers, peeled and spiralized

1 daikon, peeled and spiralized

2 onions, sliced

half cup sunflower seeds

2 tbsp. sesame seeds

4 tbsp. linseed oil (flaxseed oil or flax oil)

2 tbsp. pomegranate seeds

Dressing:

4 tbsp. cream

4 tbsp. soy sauce

4 cloves of garlic

salt and pepper

How to Prepare:

1. Preheat the oven and roast the sunflower seeds in the oven for 5 min. until lightly browned and crispy.

2. In a bowl, sprinkle the onions with the salt and pour the linseeds oil and then place the sliced onions in the fridge for one hour.

3. Combine the cucumbers and daikon stripes.

4. Let's get to the dressing now – combine the cream, soy sauce, garlic, salt, and pepper and pulse them in a blender until homogenous mass.

5. Mix the dressing with the cucumbers and daikon spaghetti and spoon some sesame seeds and pomegranate seeds on top!

Nutritional Information:

Calories: 147

Total fat: 10 oz

Total carbohydrates: 16 oz

Protein: 7 oz

Inspiralized Chicken and Oranges

Prep Time: 10 min. | Cooking Time: 20 min. | Servings: 2

Ingredients:

2 chicken breasts

1 ripe orange

1 zucchini, peeled and spiralized

4 oz lettuce

1 onion

5 tbsp. Olive oil

5 tbsp. lemon juice

salt and pepper

How to Prepare:

1. Heat the water and boil the chicken breasts for 20 min. until soft.

2. Peel the orange and then cut it into cubes and then slice the chicken breasts.

3. Chop the lettuce and onion and combine them with the orange cubes, zucchini, and sliced chicken breasts.

4. Sprinkle the salt and pepper and pour the Olive oil and lemon juice over the salad and you are free to serve!

Nutritional Information:

Calories: 187

Total fat: 14 oz

Total carbohydrates: 23 oz

Protein: 10 oz

Inspiralized Zucchini and Turkey Bruschetta

Prep Time: 10 min. | Cooking Time: 30 min. | Servings: 4

Ingredients:

2 turkey breasts, sliced

1 zucchini, peeled and spiralized

4 garlic cloves, chopped

5 tbsp. Olive oil

half cup pesto sauce

salt

Dressing:

4 tomatoes, cubed

4 garlic cloves

4 tbsp. soy sauce

10 fresh basil leaves, chopped

salt and pepper

How to Prepare:

1. Marinate the turkey breasts slices in the pesto sauce and 4 chopped garlic cloves with the salt overnight.

2. Heat the Olive oil in a frying pan or wok and fry the turkey breasts for 20 min. until soft, flipping half-way through frying. Both turkey slices sides should be completely cooked and lightly browned.

3. Add the zucchini stripes and stew with the closed lid for 10 minutes more until the liquid is absorbed.

4. Let's get to the bruschetta dressing now – combine the tomatoes, garlic, basil leaves, salt, and pepper and pour the soy sauce and then place in the fridge for few hours.

5. Top each turkey slice with the zucchini stripes and bruschetta and serve warm.

Nutritional Information:

Calories: 247

Total fat: 19 oz

Total carbohydrates: 33 oz

Protein: 15 oz

Inspiralized Mango Salad

 Prep Time: 10 min. | Servings: 2

Ingredients:

1 mango

4 lettuce

half cup raisins

4 tbsp. arugula

4 tbsp. orange juice

4 tbsp. liquid honey

How to Prepare:

1. Peel and spiralize the mango and then chop the lettuce and arugula and combine with the mango.

2. Pour the orange juice and liquid honey over the salad.

3. Place the mango salad in the fridge for 1 hour and then serve.

Nutritional Information:

Calories: 155

Total fat: 5 oz

Total carbohydrates: 15 oz

Protein: 7 oz

Spiralized Cucumber and Pine Nuts

 Prep Time: 5 min. | Cooking Time: 10 min. | Servings: 2

Ingredients:

1 cup pine nuts

1 cup cream

1 cucumber, peeled and spiralized

3 tomatoes, cubed

5 oz lettuce, chopped

2 onions, chopped

5 tbsp. Olive oil

parsley, chopped

Dressing:

5 tbsp. Olive oil

4 tbsp. soy sauce

4 tbsp. lemon juice

10 fresh basil leaves

salt and pepper

How to Prepare:

1. Roast the pine nuts in the oven for 10 min. until lightly browned and crispy.

2. In a bowl, sprinkle the onions with the salt and pour the Olive oil and then place the onions in the fridge for one hour.

3. Combine all the vegetables in a bowl and spoon the cream on top.

4. Let's get to the dressing now - pulse all the dressing ingredients in a blender until they have a smooth and creamy consistency.

5. Place the dressing in the fridge for 1 hour.

6. Pour the dressing over the salad and mix well, and then you are free to serve!

Nutritional Information:

Calories: 146

Total fat: 12 oz

Total carbohydrates: 23 oz

Protein: 7 oz

Inspiralized Beets and Apples Salad

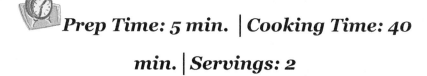 **Prep Time: 5 min. | Cooking Time: 40 min. | Servings: 2**

Ingredients:

2 medium beets

half cup walnuts

2 sour apples

half cup dried apricots, cubed

salt and pepper

fresh parsley, chopped

Dressing:

4 tbsp. Olive oil

4 tbsp. vegan mayonnaise

4 tbsp. mustard

salt

How to Prepare:

1. Roast the walnuts in the oven for 10 min. until lightly browned and crispy.

2. Heat the water and boil the beets in a saucepan over medium heat for 30 min. until soft.

3. Cool the beets by placing them in the cold water for 10 min. and then peel and spiralize them.

4. Peel the apples and then spiralize them.

5. In a bowl, combine the beets, apples, apricots, salt, pepper and chopped parsley.

6. Let's prepare the dressing now - pulse all the dressing ingredients in a blender until they have a smooth and creamy consistency.

7. Combine the dressing with the salad and walnuts and then mix well.

8. Place the beets and raisins salad in the fridge for 1 hour and then serve.

Nutritional Information:

Calories: 165

Total fat: 12 oz

Total carbohydrates: 25 oz

Protein: 9 oz

Walnuts Zucchini Spaghetti

Prep Time: 5 min. | Cooking Time: 10 min. | Servings: 3

Ingredients:

1 young zucchini, peeled and spiralized

half cup walnuts

1 avocado, sliced

2 cucumbers, peeled and spiralized

Dressing:

4 tbsp. white wine vinegar

4 tbsp. soy sauce

4 cloves of garlic

5 fresh basil leaves

salt and pepper

How to Prepare:

1. Roast the walnuts in the oven for 10 min. until lightly browned and crispy.

2. Spiralize the zucchini and cucumbers or grate them in Korean style using a Korean carrot grater.

3. Combine the vegetables and half of the avocado with the walnuts.

4. Let's prepare the dressing now – pulse the white wine vinegar, soy sauce, garlic, salt, pepper, basil leaves and remaining avocado in a blender until homogenous green mass.

5. Pour the dressing over the zucchini and cucumbers spaghetti and serve!

Nutritional Information:

Calories: 157

Total fat: 14 oz

Total carbohydrates: 24 oz

Protein: 10 oz

Potato Strips in Dressing

 Prep Time: 5 min. │ Cooking Time: 10 min. │ Servings: 2

Ingredients:

4 potatoes, peeled and spiralized

1 tbsp. Herbes de Provence

1 tsp. dried basil

1 cup Olive oil

Dressing:

half cup cream

5 oz spinach

4 garlic cloves, chopped

5 tbsp. mayonnaise

5 tbsp. garlic sauce

salt and pepper

parsley, chopped

How to Prepare:

1. Heat the oil and fry the potatoes for 10 minutes until crisp.

2. Let's prepare the dressing now – pulse the cream, spinach, mayonnaise, garlic, garlic sauce, salt, and pepper in a blender until homogenous mass.

3. Pour the dressing over the potatoes and sprinkle with the spices and parsley and you are free to serve.

Nutritional Information:

Calories: 245

Total fat: 18 oz

Total carbohydrates: 38 oz

Protein: 9 oz

Zucchini Pasta with Shrimps and Garlic

 Prep Time: 5 min. | Cooking Time: 25 min. | Servings: 4

Ingredients:

2 zucchinis, peeled and spiralized

8 cloves of garlic, chopped

8 shrimps, peeled

4 slices of bacon, smoked

7 tbsp. mayonnaise

4 tbsp. Olive oil

salt and pepper

bunch of parsley, chopped

How to Prepare:

1. Heat the oil in a skillet and fry the bacon for 5 min. and flip on the other side and fry for 5 min more until crisp.

2. Add the garlic and zucchinis and stew for 5 minutes and then set aside with the closed lid.

3. Season the shrimps with the salt and pepper and boil for 10 minutes.

4. Combine the shrimps with the bacon and vegetables in a skillet.

5. Transfer to a plate and spoon the mayonnaise and garnish with the parsley on top to serve!

Nutritional Information:

Calories: 263

Total fat: 35 oz

Total carbohydrates: 47 oz

Protein: 19 oz

Mediterranean Spiralized Cucumbers

 Prep Time: 10 min. | Servings: 2

Ingredients:

4 cucumbers, peeled and spiralized

1 cup cherry tomatoes, halved

1 onion, chopped

1 cup black olives, pitted

5 tbsp. Olive oil

1 cup Feta cheese, crumbled

2 tbsp. lemon juice

salt and pepper

How to Prepare:

1. Combine the cucumbers with the cherry tomatoes, onion, and olives.

2. Pour the Olive oil and lemon juice over the vegetables and add the crumbled Feta cheese on top to serve in few plates.

Nutritional Information:

Calories: 195

Total fat: 15 oz

Total carbohydrates: 25 oz

Protein: 12 oz

Spicy Pumpkin Noodles

 Prep Time: 10 min. | *Cooking Time: 10 min.* | *Servings: 4*

Ingredients:

1 young pumpkin, peeled and spiralized

1 cup pumpkin seeds

1 cucumber, peeled and spiralized

2 tomatoes, chopped

Dressing:

1 tbsp. chili pepper powder

4 tbsp. white wine vinegar

4 cloves of garlic

10 fresh basil leaves

salt and pepper

How to Prepare:

1. Roast the pumpkin seeds in the oven for 10 min. until lightly browned and crispy.

2. Combine the spiralized pumpkin, cucumber, tomatoes and pumpkin seeds.

3. Let's prepare the dressing now – pulse the white wine vinegar, garlic, salt, pepper and basil leaves in a blender until homogenous mass.

4. Spoon the dressing over the pumpkin noodles and serve!

Nutritional Information:

Calories: 147

Total fat: 13 oz

Total carbohydrates: 23 oz

Protein: 9 oz

Spiralized Potatoes with Cheese

Prep Time: 10 min. │ Cooking Time: 30 min. │ Servings: 2

Ingredients:

5 potatoes, peeled and spiralized

5 oz Parmesan cheese, grated

4 tomatoes, cubed

1 onion, chopped

7 tbsp. sunflower oil

1 tbsp. powdered garlic

1 tsp. powdered cayenne pepper

salt and pepper

How to Cook:

1. Season the potatoes with the powdered garlic, salt, pepper and cayenne pepper and toss in the sunflower oil.

2. Preheat the oven to 280°-300° Fahrenheit and bake the potatoes for 20 min. until crispy.

3. Add the tomatoes and onion and cook for 10 min. more

4. Sprinkle the Parmesan cheese on top and serve.

Nutritional Information:

Calories: 242

Total fat: 17 oz

Total carbohydrates: 26 oz

Proteins: 11 oz

Zucchini Zoodles with Tomatoes

Prep Time: 10 min. | **Cooking Time: 20 min.** | **Servings: 2**

Ingredients:

2 zucchinis, peeled and spiralized

1 cup cherry tomatoes, halved

2 carrots, peeled and spiralized

1 onion, chopped

5 cloves of garlic, chopped

5 tbsp. white flour

5 tbsp. sesame seeds oil

Oregano, dried

salt and pepper

parsley, chopped

How to Cook:

1. Toss the zucchinis and carrots in the oregano, garlic salt, and pepper mix.

2. Heat the oil in a skillet and fry the zucchinis, onions, and carrots for 10 min.

3. Add the tomatoes and spoon the white flour and stew for 10 min. with the closed lid.

4. Sprinkle the vegetables with the chopped parsley and transfer to plates to serve.

Nutritional Information:

Calories: 150

Total fat: 11 oz

Total carbohydrates: 21 oz

Protein: 8 oz

Inspiralized Carrots with Hake

 Prep Time: 10 min. | Cooking Time: 35 min. | Servings: 4

Ingredients:

4 carrots, peeled and spiralized

3 hakes, frozen

2 big onions, chopped

4 tbsp. white flour

8 tbsp. sunflower oil

half cup raisins

salt and pepper

How to Cook:

1. Unfreeze the hake first. Leave it in a bowl for overnight in the fridge or in a room temperature. If you want to unfreeze it fast then consider defrosting it in the microwave.

2. Heat the oil in a deep skillet or wok and fry the fish for 15 min.

3. Spoon the carrots, onions, and raisins and then mix in the white flour.

4. Stew the hake and vegetables with the closed lid for 20 min. and then serve warm.

Nutritional Information:

Calories: 299

Total fat: 24 oz

Total carbohydrates: 33 oz

Protein: 14 oz

Spiralized Cheese Pasta with Garlic

 Prep Time: 10 min. | Servings: 2

Ingredients:

5 oz Cheddar or Parmesan cheese

8 garlic cloves, chopped

8 tbsp. mayonnaise

2 tbsp. mustard

salt and pepper

How to Cook:

1. Spiralize the Cheddar or Parmesan cheese and combine it with the garlic.

2. In a bowl, combine the cheese with the mayonnaise and mustard and mix well.

3. Sprinkle the cheese pasta with the salt and pepper and place in the fridge for 2 hours and then serve.

Nutritional Information:

Calories: 214

Total fat: 29 oz

Total carbohydrates: 38 oz

Protein: 15 oz

Baked Pumpkin and Potatoes Zoodles

Prep Time: 10 min. | **Cooking Time: 40 min.**
| **Servings: 4**

Ingredients:

15 oz pumpkin, peeled and spiralized

1 mango, cubed

2 potatoes, peeled and spiralized

1 big onion, chopped

4 tsp. garlic powder

7 tbsp. Olive oil

2 tbsp. lemon juice

salt and pepper

How to Prepare:

1. Season the pumpkin and potatoes with the powdered garlic, salt, and pepper and toss in the Olive oil.

2. Preheat the oven to 280°-300° Fahrenheit and bake the pumpkin with the potatoes, mango, and onion for 40 min. until the pumpkin is golden brown, caramelized and soft.

3. Sprinkle the vegetables with the lemon juice and serve.

Nutritional Information:

Calories: 178

Total fat: 15 oz

Total carbohydrates: 21 oz

Protein: 7 oz

Spiralized Potatoes Fries with Pineapple

 Prep Time: 8 min. | Cooking Time: 40 min. | Servings: 5

Ingredients:

1 lb potatoes, peeled and spiralized

half pineapple, cubed

4 carrots

1 red onion

fresh greens

Sauce:

5 tbsp. white wine vinegar

5 tbsp. white flour

4 tsp. garlic powder

Herbes de Provence

salt and pepper

How to Cook:

1. Steam all the vegetables to half-cooked and set aside.

2. Let's prepare the sauce now – combine the white wine vinegar with the garlic powder and flour and cook for 5 min. mixing all the time. Remember that it is crucial to avoid browning of the white flour.

3. Stirring constantly bring the mixture to a boil.

4. Mix in the garlic powder, Herbes de Provence, salt and pepper and then combine with the vegetables, close the lid and set aside.

5. Preheat the oven to 300°-320° Fahrenheit and bake all the vegetables and pineapple cubes with the sauce for 35 min. until the potatoes are soft.

6. Sprinkle the fresh greens on top and serve.

Nutritional Information:

Calories: 220

Total fat: 22 oz

Total carbohydrates: 29 oz

Protein: 9 oz

Spiralized Zucchini Noodles Soup with Turkey

 Prep Time: 10 min. | Cooking Time: 1 h. 10 min. | Servings: 4

Ingredients:

1 lb. turkey breast, cubed

1 zucchini, spiralized

1 seeded Cayenne pepper

8 garlic cloves, chopped

2 onions, chopped

2 carrots, chopped

1 celery, chopped

half tsp. cayenne pepper

2 tbsp. garlic powder

salt and pepper

How to Prepare:

1. Season the turkey breast with the salt and pepper and leave for few hours.

2. Place the turkey breast into the saucepan and add all the ingredients except for the spiralized zucchini and then boil it for about 1 hour.

3. Mix in the zucchini noodles and cook for 10 min. more with the closed lid until the zucchini is soft.

4. Serve warm with the cream.

Nutritional Information:

Calories: 225

Total fat: 20 oz

Total carbohydrates: 34 oz

Protein: 11 oz

Zucchini Pasta Soup with Dried Mushrooms

Prep Time: 10 min. | **Cooking Time: 1-hour**
| **Servings: 4**

Ingredients:

1 cup of porcini mushrooms, dried

1 zucchini, peeled and spiralized

2 tbsp. bacon grease

5 garlic cloves, chopped

2 onions, chopped

2 carrots, chopped

1 celery, chopped

2 tbsp. garlic powder

1 tbsp. chili powder

salt and pepper

How to Prepare:

1. Soak the dried porcini mushrooms in water and leave for few hours.

2. Place the mushrooms into the saucepan and add all the ingredients except for the spiralized zucchini and then boil it for about 50 min.

3. Mix in the zucchini noodles and cook for 10 min. more with the closed lid until the zucchini is soft.

4. Serve warm with the cream.

Nutritional Information:

Calories: 193

Total fat: 21 oz

Total carbohydrates: 30 oz

Protein: 10 oz

Inspiralized Carrots with Beef

 Prep Time: 10 min. │ Cooking Time: 1-hour │ Servings: 4

Ingredients:

4 carrots, peeled and spiralized

5 oz beef, cubed

3 big onions, chopped

4 tbsp. white flour

8 tbsp. Olive oil

half cup raisins

basil, dried

salt, and pepper

How to Cook:

1. Season the beef with the basil, salt, and pepper and leave for overnight.
2. Heat the Olive oil in a deep skillet or wok and fry the beef chunks for 20 min.
3. Spoon the carrots, onions, and raisins and then mix in the white flour.
4. Stew the beef and vegetables with the closed lid for 40 min. and then serve warm.

Nutritional Information:

Calories: 308

Total fat: 25 oz

Total carbohydrates: 36 oz

Protein: 15 oz

Spiralized Vegetable Mix

 Prep Time: 10 min. | *Servings: 2*

Ingredients:

2 carrots, peeled and spiralized

1 cucumber, peeled and spiralized

1 red bell pepper, spiralized

1 yellow bell pepper, spiralized

1 orange bell pepper, spiralized

1 big red onion, peeled and spiralized

6 tbsp. Olive oil

5 tbsp. soy sauce

1 tbsp. Oregano

salt and pepper

How to Prepare:

1. In a bowl, combine all the spiralized vegetables.

2. Pour the Olive oil and soy sauce on top and sprinkle with the spices to serve.

3. Serve with the buckwheat or whole grain bread.

Nutritional Information:

Calories: 149

Total fat: 15 oz

Total carbohydrates: 22 oz

Protein: 7 oz

Peanuts and Zucchini Pasta

Prep Time: 10 min. | Cooking Time: 35 min. | Servings: 4

Ingredients:

1 zucchini, peeled and spiralized

1 cup peanuts

4 tbsp. peanut butter

4 carrots, peeled and spiralized

4 cloves of garlic

4 tbsp. Olive oil

salt and pepper

How to Cook:

1. Boil the water and cook the zucchini pasta for 10 min. Add 1 tablespoon Olive oil.

2. Roast the peanuts in the oven for 10 min. until lightly browned and crispy.

3. Pulse the garlic, salt, and pepper in a blender until smooth.

4. Heat the oil and fry the carrots for 10 min.

5. Melt the peanut butter in a skillet for 5 min. and combine with the garlic mixture and mix well.

6. Spoon the zucchini pasta into the bowl, add the garlic mixture, spoon the carrots, sprinkle with the peanuts and serve!

Nutritional Information:

Calories: 213

Total fat: 15 oz

Total carbohydrates: 23 oz

Protein: 9 oz

Zucchini Spaghetti with Avocado

 Prep Time: 5 min. | Cooking Time: 10 min. | Servings: 2

Ingredients:

2 young zucchinis, spiralized

1 avocado

2 tbsp. cream

1 can of canned corns

4 tbsp. lemon juice

10 fresh basil leaves

5 tbsp. Olive oil

salt and pepper

Herbes de Provence

How to Cook:

1. Boil the water and cook the zucchini spaghetti for 10 min. Add 1 tablespoon oil.

2. Add 2 tablespoons Olive oil when the spaghetti is ready.

3. Let's get to the sauce now – cut the avocado into pieces and pulse it with the cream, basil leaves and spices using a blender, then add some water and your sauce is ready.

4. Mix the zucchini spaghetti with the avocado sauce and stir well.

5. Add the canned corns, few basil leaves and pour the lemon juice on top to serve.

Nutritional Information:

Calories: 182

Total fat: 12 oz

Total carbohydrates: 20 oz

Protein: 8 oz

Cream Zucchini Pasta

 Prep Time: 10 min. | Cooking Time: 36 min. | Servings: 4

Ingredients:

1 fresh zucchini, spiralized

1 fresh broccoli

8 cloves of garlic, chopped

5 tbsp. milk

5 tbsp. cream

2 red onions, chopped

4 fresh tomatoes

4 tbsp. white flour

2 tbsp. mayonnaise

6 tbsp. pumpkin seeds oil

salt and pepper

How to Cook:

1. Boil the water and cook the zucchini pasta for 10 min. Add 1 tablespoon oil. In parallel, boil the broccoli to half-cooked.

2. Heat the oil and fry the red onions for 10 min. until clear.

3. In the same oil with onions, fry the garlic for 1 min on a medium heat.

4. Add the white flour, milk, cream, and mayonnaise and stir well.

5. Boil the sauce over medium heat for 10 min., don't forget to stir all the time.

6. Add the salt and pepper and close the lid and leave for 5 min., so that the sauce absorbs the flour.

7. Put the zucchini pasta into a bowl and spoon the sauce on top.

8. Half the tomatoes and put them on a plate with the zucchini pasta and serve!

Nutritional Information:

Calories: 256

Total fat: 13 oz

Total carbohydrates: 35 oz

Protein: 9 oz

Pesto, Chicken and Zucchini Pasta

 Prep Time: 5 min. | Cooking Time: 30 min. | Servings: 4

Ingredients:

2 fresh zucchinis, peeled and spiralized

1 chicken breast, cubed

2 tbsp. pasta

1 cup walnuts

5 cloves of garlic

15 fresh basil leaves

7 tbsp. milk

5 tbsp. Olive oil

salt and pepper

How to Prepare:

1. Boil the water and cook the zucchini pasta and pasta for 10 min. Add 1 tablespoon oil.

2. Add 2 tablespoons Olive oil when the zucchini pasta is ready.

3. Heat the oil and fry the chicken chunks for 20 min.

4. Place the basil, garlic, walnuts, salt, and pepper into a food processor and blend until smooth.

5. Add 3 tablespoons Olive oil and then mix well.

6. Heat the milk in a skillet and add to the pesto sauce and mix well until homogenous mass.

7. Spoon the zucchini pasta and chicken chunks into the bowl and then add the pesto sauce and you are free to serve!

Nutritional Information:

Calories: 249

Total fat: 24 oz

Total carbohydrates: 38 oz

Protein: 10 oz

Broccoli and Beets Spaghetti

 Prep Time: 5 min. | Cooking Time: 45 min. | Servings: 2

Ingredients:

2 beets, peeled

1 fresh broccoli

8 oz whole grain bread

6 cloves of garlic, chopped

2 onions

3 tbsp. white flour

1 cup milk

7 tbsp. Olive oil

4 oz tofu

5 tbsp. white wine

salt and pepper

How to Cook:

1. Boil the water and cook the broccoli for 10 min. Add 1 tablespoon oil.

2. Spiralize beets and combine them with the salt and pepper.

3. Let's get to the sauce now - chop the onions and cube the whole grain bread.

4. Heat the oil and fry the bread for 5 min., and then add the onions, chopped garlic, and broccoli and fry for 10 min. more.

5. Spoon the flour, pour some water from the boiled broccoli and white wine and cook for 10 min.

6. Next, pour the milk and stew for 10 min. with closed lid.

7. Put the beets spaghetti into the sauce and add some salt and pepper and stir well.

8. Slice the tofu on top and you are free to serve!

Nutritional Information:

Calories: 265

Total fat: 24 oz

Total carbohydrates: 34 oz

Protein: 10 oz

Beetroot and Squash Pesto Spaghetti

 Prep Time: 5 min. | *Cooking Time: 5 min.* | *Servings: 2*

Ingredients:

1 beetroot, peeled

1 squash, peeled

5 garlic cloves

10 fresh basil leaves

5 oz Mozzarella cheese, crumbled

5 tbsp. Olive oil

2 tbsp. lemon juice

salt and pepper

Herbs de Provence

How to Prepare:

1. Spiralize the beetroot and the squash.

2. Place the spiralized beetroot and squash into the microwave for 5 min. and heat until soft.

3. Pour the lemon juice and Olive oil and sprinkle the spices.

4. At this stage, you can place the basil, garlic, salt, and pepper into a blender and pulse until smooth.

5. Spoon the pesto sauce over the beetroot and squash spaghetti and sprinkle the Mozzarella cheese on top to serve.

Nutritional Information:

Calories: 175

Total fat: 21 oz

Total carbohydrates: 30 oz

Protein: 10 oz

Parsnip Noodles with Sardines

 Prep Time: 5 min. | Cooking Time: 25 min. | Servings: 4

Ingredients:

5 parsnips, peeled and spiralized

2 cans sardines in oil

2 red onions, chopped

5 garlic cloves, chopped

1 cup cherry tomatoes

5 tbsp. black Kalamata olives

5 tbsp. butter

1 tbsp. Oregano

salt and pepper

How to Prepare:

1. Heat the butter and fry the parsnips for 15 min. until soft and remove from a frying pan.

2. Fry the onions and garlic for 10 min. until clear and soft.

3. Mash the sardines with the fork and combine them with the onions, garlic, tomatoes, and Kalamata olives.

4. Add the parsnip noodles, sprinkle the Oregano, salt, and pepper and mix well to serve.

Nutritional Information:

Calories: 167

Total fat: 17 oz

Total carbohydrates: 32 oz

Protein: 12 oz

Baked Zucchini Noodles with Buckwheat

 Prep Time: 5 min. │Cooking Time: 35 min.

│Servings: 2

Ingredients:

2 bowls of peeled and spiralized zucchini

1 cup of buckwheat

10 oz Parmesan cheese, cubed

7 tbsp. Olive oil

4 tbsp. Cheddar cheese, grated

2 tbsp. garlic powder

salt and pepper

How to Prepare:

1. Boil the water and cook the buckwheat for 15 min. Add 1 tablespoon oil.

2. Add 2 tablespoons Olive oil when the buckwheat is ready.

3. Spoon the zucchini, buckwheat, Parmesan cheese, and garlic powder into a baking dish and mix.

4. Pour the Olive oil and sprinkle salt and pepper on top.

5. Preheat the oven to 280°-300° Fahrenheit and bake the zucchini mixture for 20 min. until golden.

6. 5 min. before the zucchini is ready open the oven and sprinkle with the Cheddar cheese and then serve.

Nutritional Information:

Calories: 164

Total fat: 22 oz

Total carbohydrates: 31 oz

Protein: 10 oz

Spicy Spiralized Zucchini with Rice

Prep Time: 5 min. | Cooking Time: 40 min.

| Servings: 2

Ingredients:

2 bowls of peeled and spiralized zucchini

1 cup of white rice

1 cup Feta cheese, crumbled

4 tbsp. Olive oil

4 tbsp. Parmesan cheese, grated

2 tbsp. chili powder

salt and pepper

How to Prepare:

1. Wash the rice several times and then boil the water and cook the rice for 15 min. or follow the cooking time suggested on the packet.

2. Add 2 tablespoons Olive oil when the buckwheat is ready.

3. Spoon the zucchini, rice, Feta cheese, and chili powder into a baking dish and mix.

4. Pour the Olive oil and sprinkle salt and pepper on top.

5. Preheat the oven to 280°-300° Fahrenheit and bake the zucchini mixture for 20 min. until golden.

6. 5 min. before the zucchini is ready open the oven and sprinkle with the Parmesan cheese and then serve.

Nutritional Information:

Calories: 167

Total fat: 21 oz

Total carbohydrates: 32 oz

Protein: 12 oz

Baked Zucchini Noodles with Beef

Prep Time: 5 min. | *Cooking Time: 1 h.*

| *Servings: 2*

Ingredients:

4 cups of peeled and spiralized zucchini

5 oz beef, minced

1 cup of peeled and spiralized carrots

2 onions, chopped

1 cup Mozzarella cheese, sliced

8 tbsp. Olive oil

2 tbsp. chili powder

salt and pepper

parsley, chopped

How to Prepare:

1. Heat the oil and fry the minced bacon for 15 min. until golden brown and then close the lid and stew for 15 min. until beef is soft.

2. Spoon the zucchini, carrots, onions, beef, and chili powder into a baking dish and mix.

3. Pour the Olive oil and sprinkle salt and pepper on top.

4. Preheat the oven to 280°-300° Fahrenheit and bake the zucchini mixture for 30 min. until soft.

5. 5 min. before the zucchini is ready open the oven and place the Mozzarella cheese slices on top and then serve.

Nutritional Information:

Calories: 264

Total fat: 29 oz

Total carbohydrates: 40 oz

Protein: 15 oz

Eggplant Spaghetti with Pesto

Prep Time: 5 min. | Cooking Time: 20 min. | Servings: 2

Ingredients:

2 eggplants, peeled and spiralized

1 cup of peeled and spiralized carrots

1 cup mushrooms, champignons (cubed)

2 onions, chopped

8 garlic cloves

15 fresh basil leaves

1 cup Cheddar cheese, grated

8 tbsp. Olive oil

2 tbsp. garlic powder

salt and pepper

How to Prepare:

1. Sprinkle the eggplant with the salt and leave it for 30 min. and then pour 2 tbsp. Olive oil.

2. Heat the oil and fry the eggplants, carrots, mushrooms, and onions for 20 min. until clear.

3. Place the basil, garlic, salt, and pepper into a blender and pulse until smooth.

4. Pour the pesto sauce over the eggplants and sprinkle with the garlic powder, salt, and pepper on top.

5. Sprinkle the Cheddar cheese on top and then serve.

Nutritional Information:

Calories: 244

Total fat: 24 oz

Total carbohydrates: 36 oz

Protein: 14 oz

Spiralized Zucchini with Onions

 Prep Time: 5 min. | Cooking Time: 30 min. | Servings: 2

Ingredients:

2 zucchinis, peeled and spiralized

4 onions, peeled and spiralized

8 tbsp. Olive oil

5 tbsp. soy sauce

2 tbsp. garlic powder

1 tbsp. sesame seeds

salt and pepper

How to Prepare:

1. Heat the oil in the frying pan or wok and fry the onions for 10 min. on a medium heat until clear.
2. Mix in the zucchini stripes, garlic powder, salt, and pepper, and then close the lid and stew for 20 min.
3. Pour the soy sauce and sprinkle with the sesame seeds on top to serve.

Nutritional Information:

Calories: 159

Total fat: 18 oz

Total carbohydrates: 30 oz

Protein: 10 oz

Spiralized Beetroots with Mackerel

 Prep Time: 5 min. | Cooking Time: 10 min. | Servings: 2

Ingredients:

2 beetroots, peeled and spiralized

1 big mackerel, smoked

2 onions, peeled and spiralized

8 tbsp. Olive oil

5 tbsp. mayonnaise

2 tbsp. garlic powder

salt and pepper

How to Prepare:

1. Heat the oil in the frying pan or wok and fry the onions for 10 min. on a medium heat until clear.
2. Cut the mackerel into pieces and mash with a fork.

3. Combine the mackerel with the beetroot stripes, mayonnaise, garlic powder, onions, salt and pepper to serve.

Nutritional Information:

Calories: 169

Total fat: 22 oz

Total carbohydrates: 32 oz

Protein: 11 oz

Walnuts and Zucchini Pasta

 Prep Time: 5 min. | *Cooking Time: 35 min.*

| *Servings: 2*

Ingredients:

2 medium zucchinis, peeled and spiralized

4 slices of bacon

1 cup of walnuts

1 cup dried tomatoes

2 garlic cloves, chopped

10 fresh basil leaves, chopped

5 tbsp. Olive oil

5 tbsp. mayonnaise

salt and pepper

How to Prepare:

1. Roast the walnuts in the oven for 10 min. until lightly browned and crispy.

2. Heat the oil in the frying pan or wok and fry the zucchini stripes for 10 min. on a medium heat until clear and then add the bacon slices and fry for 5 min.

3. Add in the walnuts, tomatoes, garlic, mayonnaise, salt and pepper, and stew with the closed lid for 10 min.

4. Transfer to plates and sprinkle with the chopped basil leaves on top to serve.

Nutritional Information:

Calories: 224

Total fat: 23 oz

Total carbohydrates: 42 oz

Protein: 15 oz

Beetroots Noodles with Bacon

 Prep Time: 5 min. | Cooking Time: 30 min.
| Servings: 2

Ingredients:

2 beetroots, peeled and spiralized

5 slices of bacon

1 cup tomatoes, halved

2 garlic cloves, chopped

half cup Feta cheese, crumbled

5 tbsp. Olive oil

salt and pepper

fresh dill, chopped

How to Prepare:

1. Heat the oil in the frying pan and fry the bacon slices on medium heat until crisp for around 10 min.

2. Fry the beetroots separately for 5 min. and then stew with the closed lid for 5 min. more.

3. Combine the beets with the tomatoes, garlic, salt and pepper and stew with the closed lid for 10 min.

4. Transfer to plates and add the bacon slices, Feta cheese, and fresh dill on top to serve.

Nutritional Information:

Calories: 214

Total fat: 24 oz

Total carbohydrates: 45 oz

Protein: 15 oz

Kohlrabi Noodles with Beef

 Prep Time: 5 min. | Cooking Time: 35 min. | Servings: 2

Ingredients:

2 kohlrabis, peeled and spiralized

5 oz beef, cubed

2 onions, spiralized

2 garlic cloves, chopped

half cup Cheddar cheese, grated

5 tbsp. Olive oil

salt and pepper

How to Prepare:

1. Heat the oil in the frying pan or wok and fry the beef chunks on medium heat for around 15 min. until they become crispy.

2. Remove the beef chunks and fry the onions for 10 min. until clear.

3. Add in the kohlrabi stripes, garlic, salt and pepper, and stew with the closed lid for 10 min.

4. Mix in the beef chunks and stir well.

5. Transfer to plates and sprinkle the Cheddar cheese on top to serve.

Nutritional Information:

Calories: 234

Total fat: 22 oz

Total carbohydrates: 46 oz

Protein: 14 oz

Cucumbers Pasta Rolls

Prep Time: 5 min. | Servings: 2

Ingredients:

2 cucumbers, peeled and spiralized

5 tbsp. hummus

6 turkey slices, smoked

2 garlic cloves, crushed

5 tbsp. mayonnaise

half cup soy sauce

salt and pepper

How to Prepare:

1. Spoon and spread the hummus on each turkey slice.

2. Add the cucumber stripes, mayonnaise and garlic on top.

3. Wrap the turkey slices around each cucumber mixture ball securing it with a wooden toothpick.

4. Pour the soy sauce on top to serve or use the soy sauce as a dipping sauce.

<u>Nutritional Information:</u>

Calories: 129

Total fat: 20 oz

Total carbohydrates: 28 oz

Protein: 12 oz

Conclusion

Thank you for buying this spiralizer cookbook. I hope this cookbook was able to help you to prepare delicious spiralizer recipes.

If you've enjoyed this book, I'd greatly appreciate if you could leave an honest review on Amazon.

Reviews are very important to us authors, and it only takes a minute for you to post.

Your direct feedback could be used to help other readers to discover the advantages of spiralizer recipes!

Thank you again and I hope you have enjoyed this cookbook.

Other Cookbooks by Brendan Fawn

Keto Fat Bombs

Keto Fat Bombs: Keto Desserts

Keto Fat Bombs: Chocolate Fat Bomb Recipes

Keto Desserts

Plant Based Diet

Veg Recipes

Bread Machine Cookbook

Homemade Pasta Cookbook

Vegetarian Cookbook for Beginners

Printed in Great Britain
by Amazon

74688462R00059